dedication

This book is dedicated to my lovely daughter, Penelope. Without her arrival, I would have never been so inspired to care about nutrition and healthy eating or experienced scrambling to find a way to logistically get healthy, Real Food dinners on the table every night.

chapter outline

foreword

Matt Hagel

Chef of Miccosukee Root Cellar,
a Farm-to-Table cafe in Tallahassee, FL

Growing up, I remember always watching or being a part of my mother's and grandmother's cooking, but it never occurred to me that it would become my career and passion. Now in my thirties, I understand how important the family meal is. It is a chance for all of us to get together and talk about our day or problems, a chance for us to commune as a family. My mother insisted on us being together for this meal since breakfast and lunch were usually spent separate due to schedules. My father had to work until 7 or 8pm, so we usually ate late, but no matter what, we were always together for those few moments.

Now 16 years into the professional culinary world, I have experienced many changes, many different environments, and have worn many hats. I started my career in the corporate world, growing and training in an environment more focused on dollars than quality of products. Moving into mom-and-pop restaurants, I found that the love was more prevalent in these private establishments. The variety of these experiences gave me a well-rounded training and opened my eyes to more aspects of the field.

I began to focus on where my food came from, who grew it, and what their practices were. Currently, I have relationships with over a dozen farmers and have seen firsthand the dedication and passion they put into their products. Farmers live and die with their crops and livestock and have to be involved 100%. In turn, I have found a gratitude for and satisfaction with the products I work with everyday.

The small farms don't usually make a huge profit, but it's about more than just dollars. A farmer is like an artist, proud of their painting. They love to talk and educate everyone on their product, how they grow, the practices they use, and how they harvest. Get to know your farmer and see where your food comes from. If you have any interest in gardening, all you have do is go to a local farmer's market and ask questions - they will talk your ear off!

Buying organic, chemical- or pesticide-free is great, but the best way to eat, the healthiest option for you and for the planet, is to eat food from local farmers. Just like you care so deeply about what you are preparing for your family, the farmers care deeply about the food they are serving to you. By knowing your farmer and your food, you know exactly what goes into the meals for your family.

I urge you all to try Stephanie's cookbook. It is full of simple, easy meals that utilize farm fresh and local foods. Eating healthy and organic can be overwhelming for some, especially folks who do not know how to cook, but her book is the perfect guide for either someone looking to completely overhaul their food choices or for someone who wants to take baby steps and integrate new ideas slowly. Her flavors and spice combinations are simple but delicious, and above all they are comforting and nourishing for your family in a way that is efficient and cost-effective.

Up until I got pregnant with my daughter, I was the girl who could not cook. I was the girl who started fires in the kitchen and ruined entire meals. I was the girl who threw a dinner party and made a meal but it was only barely edible. I would run around the kitchen like a chicken with its head cut off. It was beyond overwhelming and stressful.

I realize now that I stayed out of the kitchen because it was painful. Every time I went into my kitchen, it brought up horrible memories of my childhood. Because of that anxiety and the feelings that would surface from my childhood when I would try to cook, I stayed out of the kitchen. I was too afraid to face my fears and kept them stuffed down for a long time. The pain of having a mother who was not emotionally available stung the most when I was in the kitchen. I could keep pushing down that pain, as long as I stayed out of the kitchen.

I think part of the reason I started cooking with a slow cooker is because I could only emotionally handle chopping up ingredients, dumping them into a slow cooker, turning it on and then running the hell out of the kitchen.

Being in the kitchen before Penelope came along brought up sad memories for me. The pain of having a mother who was neglectful and not emotionally available stung the most when I was in the kitchen. I could keep pushing that pain down as long as I stayed out of the kitchen.

To reinforce that behavior, I also ate poorly. It was as if I felt like since my own mother did not care about me enough to get her act together and make a solid, nutritious meal for me on a daily basis, then I must be of no value. I must not be important enough or lovable enough. So getting to a place where I felt I was lovable and worthy enough for the time and effort to make a healthy meal took a long time.

I started being interested in what healthy meant when I left my house at 17. At first, my interest lied in figuring out how to lose weight. Gradually, I became interested in feeling good and learning the correlation between food and health. It's been such a process for me; I started out as a vegetarian, went to being a vegan, tried carb-free, dairy-free and on and on. I feel like I have tried every health fad out there. When I found out about the Weston A. Price Foundation and Real Food, it was like coming home.

I come from a long line of farmers. My great grandparents on my father's side were German immigrants who setttled in Kansas and started a dairy farm. On my mother's side, my step-grandfather was one of the biggest tomato farmers in South Florida and they also had a large avocado grove. My own father ran a small nursery and avocado grove and we had a vegetable garden and chickens.

Farming is in my blood and from an early age I wanted to garden. I remember at age ten starting my own garden with sunflowers and radishes. I was blown away that one little seed could grow a radish! When I was older I realized I could buy food from farmers that treated their animals well instead of simply opting out.

Instead of having to boycott industrial foods and cut out meat, I could eat meat from local farms that pastured-raised their animals. I finally figured out what healthy really means. And eating this way also hits home with my passion for healing the earth. I have a degree in Environmental Science and have always cared about sustainable, chemical-free living. I wish you could have seen in me in college; a total hippy, didn't even my shave my legs.

So, on my worst days I have been thinking, "Who the hell am I to have a cookbook? Nobody cares what I have to say." On my best days, I think, "Wait a minute. My life experiences are valuable!" I finally feel confident in the kitchen. Yes, I learn something new every day, but I also have things to share!

Here is where I found my cooking point of view. I am telling a story from a beginner's point of view, and hopefully that will make me more marketable and relatable. If I can get over what was holding me back and claim my birthright to nourishing food, you can too. If I can cook, so can you.

With all my love,

Stephanie Brandt Cornais

Founder and Creative Director of Mama and Baby Love

what is real food?

I started eating organic foods when I was 19 or 20 and I have only gotten more passionate about food as the years wear on. Reading the book Nourishing Traditions by Sally Fallon, and numerous other Real Food blogs has changed my life.

The moment I heard about Real Food, my whole mind/body/soul knew that it was right and what I had spent over a decade looking for. I finally figured out what healthy meant.

I still consider myself a Real Food newbie. There are still plenty of recipes I can't make: I get mild anxiety when I make yogurt or water kefir, and I can't make kombucha to save my life, but at least I know all the basics like how to soak nuts and grains, and how to make homemade stock.

In a nutshell, Real Food is food that is, well, real. Most of the time if it comes in a bag, box or package it is not real. There are some exceptions of small companies packaging Real Food items but 90% of packaged food is not real even if it is labeled organic. Real Food is about cooking in a traditional, homemade way that makes food easier to digest so the nutrients in the food are more easily absorbed. It is about eating wild-caught seafood, and meat from animals that have been pastured and treated kindly at small farms. It is about eating full-fat raw milk, yogurt and butter. It's about eating organic fruits and vegetables, and buying them in season from local farmers whenever possible, or growing your own.

In essence, Real Food goes against the grain politically and does not agree with the USDA Food Pyramid. The good news is that once you are on board with Real Food, you will realize that all those family recipes that you thought were unhealthy are actually healthy if you focus the quality of the ingredients. Take butter, for example. Fake butter like margarine is not good for you, but real butter made from pastured cows is one of the healthiest things you can eat! So go ahead and cook with butter, plenty of it! But just make sure it's a quality butter. Buying raw butter straight from your farmer is best, but there are some good brands like Kerry Gold that can be found at most grocery chains.

Real Food is an Investment

There are a number of things you can do to be more efficient with your spending and save money, but in general Real Food just costs more, so make strides to wrap your mind around the idea of just plain spending more money on quality food. It's an investment in yourself and your future. Yes, you may spend more money on food, but it's easier if you reduce other uncessary expenses and place a higher value on your family's health. You can expect to spend about 20% of your income on food, more for larger families, which is more than double what the average American spends. Think about the health of an average American and decide what you want your health and life to be. It's an investment in yourself and your future. Yes, you may spend more money on food, but you will be reducing your medical bills in your future. Eating well is preventative health care. If your child eats well and their brain actually has a chance to operate well, they are much more likely to do well in school and get that full ride to college.

Real Food Basics

I've included the use of animal fats such as butter and lard in my recipes for the important fat soluble vitamins that they include. Contrary to popular belief, not only do these fats not cause things like heart disease or diabetes, but they're also very nutrient dense and help restore our bodies to health. In my recipes, I mostly say sautée with butter, but bacon grease, olive oil, and coconut oil are good options too.

Another big step of eating Real Food is getting to know your farmer, buying from a co-op or farmers market and buying your food directly from a farm. This is the healthiest way to eat for your body and for the earth. You are supporting your local economy too.

Could you imagine fried chicken made without shortening, but instead with real lard (with all its vitamins and nutrients!)? How wonderful a chicken tastes that had a peaceful life. The beginning step of Real Food is simply swapping out your processed ingredients for ones that are real. No fake butter, oil, low-fat, or no-fat. Buy full-fat everything. Swap out regular salt for sea salt, as it has more minerals. Using filtered water in all your cooking is another biggie in making sure your food is as healthy as possible.

Adding fermented foods is also important. Kombucha and sauerkraut are great for fermentation, as they have live enzymes and probiotics to help your digestion. You can ferment anything, from lemonade to salsa.

Most of my recipes are grain-free, gluten-free and dairy-free. The recipes that do include these ingredients are easily adaptable.

Grains are not the devil, especially if they are prepared properly, but there is a huge misconception about how much grains you need in your diet. If you look at the USDA food pyramid, grains make up the majority of the recommend diet. Really that triangle should be turned upside down, with proteins and fats making up the majority of your diet and grains being the smallest portion of your daily diet.

Grains are incredibly hard on the digestive track, which directly impacts how much nutrition is being absorbed. Worse yet, grains also contain large amounts of phytic acid, which binds minerals. Even with soaking and sprouting, eating too many grains will be a strain on the endocrine system as your body copes with digesting these tough carb-filled plant foods.

I eat about two small servings of grains a day, and that includes my dessert intake. Because I love to have bread and crackers throughout the day with a meal or snack, I tend to make all my regular meals grain and gluten-free so I am not adding additional grains to my diet.Throughout the book I suggest serving your slow cooker freezer meal with some sort of side, such as rice, cous-cous, salad or sautéed vegetables.

It may be surprising that I recommend white rice instead of brown rice. While white rice is a grain and therefore quite starchy, it is still better than brown rice if you choose to eat any rice at all. Brown rice is just a rice that still has a hull on it, but the hulls of grains are used as protection for the grain to be able to make it through the digestive tract of animals, i.e. it is not meant to be digested well. As we know, being able to digest our food is critical in being able to get nutrients out. Furthermore, the hull of brown rice also contains phytic acid, which binds what little nutrients your digestive tract can get out to begin with. Optimally you want to choose a white rice and then also soak it to get the most nutrition.

Chemical Concerns

My recipes also call for canned food sometimes. I mention the canned amounts for ease of assembly, but your best bet is to use ingredients in their fresh, whole forms. If you are able, buy food in glass jars instead of cans. Even if you buy organic canned food, those cans still have BPA in them. It's gross, I know. So do the best you can (no pun intended!) and buy food in their whole form when you are able.

While we are talking about BPA, a note about plastic bags: sometimes I get people who ask about freezing food in plastic and if that leaches chemicals into the food. As far as I know, as long as you are not heating your food in the plastic, the chemicals are not released. I am putting the meat and veggies in cold or at room temperature, not hot.

I do not recommend using the slow cooker liners that are on the market. I know it is tempting to not have to clean up your slow cooker, but heating plastic at that high of a temperature, even BPA free ones, is not a good idea, my friends.

Natural Sweeteners

I use Rapadura instead of regular white sugar. This is simply raw sugar that not been stripped of nutrients. Yes, sugar has some nutrients in it! So it's still sugar, just a little bit better for you. There are several different natural sweeteners on the market right now. I stay away from Stevia and Agave — Stevia has a funky after-taste, and Agave is no better than corn syrup as it is chemically processed. I stick with Rapadura, coconut or date sugar, shredded coconut, dates and honey.

Thickening Agents

To thicken my recipes, I use a quick-cooking tapioca or arrowroot flour. Both are healthy thickening agents for sauces and stews. Both also gluten-free. If you are in a pinch and you want to use cornstarch or regular flour, that will work as well.

Presoaking

There are several other processes to learn to make food the most digestible it can be, such as soaking grains (including rice) and beans. This is done to help reduce the amount of phytic acid in the beans. Phytic acid binds to magnesium, iron, zinc, and calcium, preventing you from absorbing the essential nutrients. The process of soaking breaks down the phytic acid and makes these nutrients more bio-available (easier for your body to absorb).

To soak dry beans or rice, simply put your selection in a big bowl or jar with room for expansion, add at least a tablespoon of an acidic medium, such as vinegar, lemon juice or fresh whey. Then fill with water to completely cover and soak overnight. If soaking almonds or other nuts, soak them in warm salt water — no acidic medium is needed. You will want to dehydrate them for 24 hours at a low teperature (between 115° and 150°) to make them crispy again.

Homemade Stock/Broth

I also mention chicken stock in many of my recipes. Homemade stock is far superior to anything you can buy in the store. It literally is one of the most nourishing foods on the planet. When I first starting cooking in a Real Food way, making stock was one of the first things I set out to do. I figured between switching to raw milk and making homemade stock, those two alone made major leaps in good health for my family and I could slowly learn the remaining traditional cooking methods as I went along. I have a great tutorial on how to make your own chicken stock on my blog.

Take Baby Steps

If you are interested in Real Food, I highly suggest you subscribe to my blog and some of the other Real Food blogs out there. Take it slow and make changes as you can, as it can be too overwhelming to try and change everything all at once. Pick one thing to change, and once you have mastered that new habit, then go to the next thing. As long as you are moving in the right direction of slowly transforming your life and the way you eat, that is what matters. One foot in front of the other, one small step at a time, always moving forward.

Assembly

Before you assemble your meals, chop all your vegetables. Sometimes I chop all the veggies the night before, or the afternoon I buy them and store them in gallon freezer bags in my fridge. The next day, I reuse the same freezer bags for the meal assembly. Like with all things I set out to accomplish, I break the task into smaller, more manageable steps.

Next, get out all your spices and other ingredients. I group them by recipe on my kitchen counter for quicker assembly. I put in all the veggies and spices first. After the veggies and spices are in, I clean up and get ready for the meat. That way I can leave the bags on the counter for a few minutes during clean-up.

Next, I add the meat. You can put the meat in a separate bag if you wish. There is no issue with combining raw veggies and raw meat if you are putting them straight into the freezer, then straight into the slow cooker the day you cook.

Sometimes I chop the meat into 1 inch cubes. Other times, I leave it whole and cut the meat up after it is cooked. I have been doing the latter more lately because I do not like handling raw meat. Grosses me out. You should see me when I am dealing with chicken heads and feet in for my stock. I breathe deep and chant, "I can do this!" to just get through it!

Many slowcooker recipes call for browning meat before adding it to the slowcooker. This is to enhance the flavor of the meat. However, in my experience, the recipe tastes the same either way, so why add an extra step?

Finally, I close the freezer bags and mix it up a little bit, then I lay it down flat so it freezes like a thin, flat brick. This saves me room in my freezer and it makes my freezer nicer to look at. I don't know about you, but I love anything lined up in a nice row or stack. I either handwrite the contents on the bag using a Sharpie pen, or I use the labels I've provided in the back of the book, which are Avery 8163 compatible.

I prefer preparing three recipes at a time because this is the most manageable for me. If you want to do one recipe at a time or 10, go right on ahead and do what works for you. I like doing three, because it only takes a couple of hours or less. Each meal gives us leftovers, and since I don't eat a slow cooker meal every day (I like to keep it varied and do simple one-dish meals once or twice a week), this is all I need to do to have a month's worth of meals in my freezer.

The whole process of assembling three recipes usually takes me a couple of hours, including clean up. The more veggies to chop, the longer it can take.

The day of cooking, I dump the contents of the bag into the slow cooker. If the contents of the bag are on the smaller side, I can usually put it in the slow cooker and get the lid on without any problems. If it is a bigger meal, I let the bag sit out for a few minutes to let it thaw just enough so I can mash it with a wooden spoon and break it up into two or three big frozen chunks (Also note that I have an All-Clad 6 quart slow cooker, which is bigger than most). Sometimes I need to cut open the gallon freezer bag, but most of the time the contents just slide out into the slow cooker.

Food Safety

The slow cooker reaches a high enough temperature while cooking that it kills any bacteria that may have gotten in while preparing your meals.

It goes without saying, but I should cover my butt and go ahead and say it: start with a clean kitchen and a clean slow cooker. If the power goes out while you are cooking your meal and you have been gone all day, just trash it — it's not worth the risk. Once you have finished cooking your meal, put leftovers in the fridge within two hours. I will usually turn it off as I am serving dinner, and leave the lid slightly ajar so it can cool down a bit before I put the leftovers in the fridge.

The USDA official recommendation is to not put frozen food into your slow cooker. I have always put my food in completely frozen and they come out great. These recipes will still work fine if you want to thaw them first and put them in your slow cooker. If you do thaw it first, thaw it in your fridge, not the counter or sink. I would recommend putting the bag on a plate or dish in your fridge, so that in case it leaks as it thaws it doesn't mess up your fridge.

Cooking Time

All the cooking times that I have listed are approximate. What I have listed is what works for me in *my* kitchen with *my* slow cooker. There are a ton of slow cookers on the market right now, all different sizes that heat differently, just like ovens. The amount of food in relation to the size of your cooker matters, so if you have too much or too little food in your cooker it can affect the outcome. So know your cooker, pay attention when you make a brand new recipe and then make notes for the next time you cook the recipe. Did you overcook it and it needs to be taken out sooner next time? Or was it a little tough and needed another hour? In general, chicken and pork cook faster than beef, but keep an eye on your meals as you get to know your cooker and get used to this style of cooking.

Servings

All of my recipes, except Opa's Empandas, Penelope's Ginger-Carrot Soup, Cumin Beans, and the Healing Chicken Soup (all of those are big and serve 6 to 8 already), have been doubled to fill two separate, gallon-sized freezer bags. **Each bag is one meal**, usually consisting of an average of 6 servings; some are more, and some are less. For my small family, that is at least one dinner and leftovers, and sometimes even two dinners and leftovers.

Split all of the listed ingredients of the recipe into two bags (with the exception of the recipes listed above). If it calls for four pounds meat, put two pounds in one bag and two in the other. If it calls for 8 cups of potatoes, put four in one bag and four in the other. The same goes for spices. You may want to mix all the spices together then evenly distribute them between the two bags, but it is not a necessary step. If a recipe calls for 8 cups of stock to be added the day of cooking, you would add 4 cups for one meal and 4 cups when you cook the second meal.

Pay attention to your label. Some recipes require adding in last minute ingredients or extra stock. Your pretty labels at the end of this cookbook will have all your reminders for you ready to go.

Kid Friendly

Any of my meals would be suitable for kids older than 10 months to eat. The slow cooker meals are awesome for babies and toddlers because the meat and veggies are so soft and easy for them to chew and digest. We did Baby-Led Weaning with Penelope, meaning she never got pureed food; We just gave her bits and pieces of whatever we were eating.

Blanching, Freezing and Cooking Vegetables

I get lots of questions about whether or not to blanch the veggies. I do not blanch my vegetables before freezing. Onions, green peppers, beets, carrots — all veggies that I cook with a lot — do not require blanching. Period. If you want to blanch the other vegetables, go right ahead.

Blanching can help improve the flavor, texture and color of the vegetable if you are sautéing or baking it, but vegetables will get very soft in the slow cooker regardless. They will get coated in the sauces or stew, obscuring those things blanching might preserve, so I figure there's no point. I also end up eating all my freezer meals within a short time period, so there is no need for blanching to help extend freezer time.

Yes, I freeze potatoes, both white and sweet. The white potatoes do change color, but it's only a marbling. It does not affect the taste of the potato at all. Again, all the veggies become covered in the sauce or stew spices, so who cares? If you do not want to freeze your potatoes, that is fine too. You can just chop them and add them the day of cooking.

Pretty much any vegetable you cook in the slow cooker is going to be mushy. If you don't like mushy vegetables, don't use your slow cooker! Alternatively, you can freeze them in a separate bag, cook them separately and mix them in after your meat is cooked. You can also try adding them to the slow cooker the last hour or half-hour of cooking and see how you like them that way.

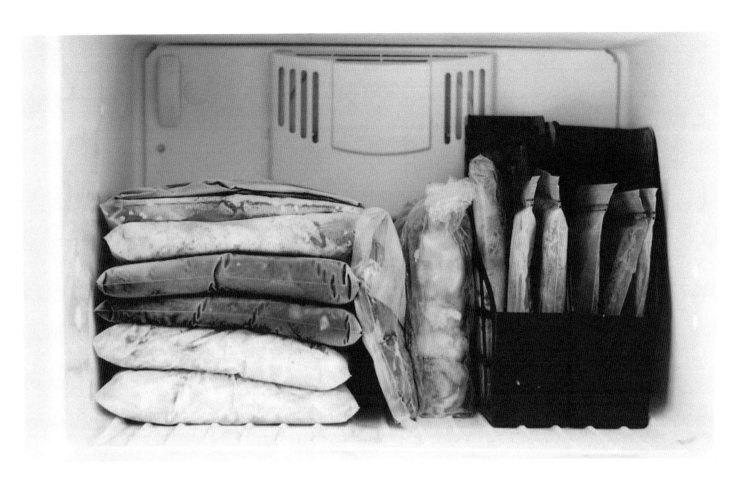

Cuts of Meat

Many of my recipes call for beef, and there are lots of different types of beef stew meat to choose from: chuck, bottom round, rump roast, and sirloin. I also use a lot of flank steak. You can use any of these cuts interchangeably for my recipes that call for beef. I always use grass-fed beef. It is so much healthier for you. It has as much omega-3s as salmon.

The majority of my recipes call for a couple pounds of meat. If you end up using a little more or a little less, that is totally fine. Chicken and pork is easy to work with, but keep in mind that they dry out more easily than beef. They can't be cooked quite as long as beef, so be extra vigilant the first time you make a new chicken or pork recipe.

Flavors and Spice

I tend not to go crazy with the spices because my husband has a sensitive stomach. I love spicy foods, so I consider these recipes to be a nice middle ground.

Since I am using high-quality ingredients, my taste buds are tuned to the subtle, rich flavors rather than the overly salty, sugary, MSG-laden processed stuff you find in cans and spice mixes. It's just like going without any sugar for a while, and then trying a piece of fruit, or even a glass of milk, and finding it far sweeter than you remember.

Also keep in mind that cooking in a slow cooker for long periods of time reduces the intensity of some spices. If you feel like your meal needs a bit more kick, I would recommend adding the spices in the last hour of cooking, instead of doubling your spices, to save money.

Wholesome and Simple

Lastly, these recipes are for your weekday family dinners. They are wholesome, nutritious and easy to prepare. They are not something amazing that you cook to impress your friends at a dinner party. This is a way to pull a meal straight from your freezer, no thawing, no second thoughts, and dump it into your slow cooker so that you can put a healthy and tasty meal on the table for your family without slaving away in the kitchen for hours on end. These meals are the workhorse of your kitchen, and the foundation of your freezer stash. They are not something that you can eat every night for an entire month. I do a one-dish freezer recipe a few nights a week. I need variation, so the rest of the week, I make pizza or tacos, eat out, etc.

These are the perfect meals for busy families, or for giving to friends and family who are ill or just had a baby. These meals are always in my freezer, so if I have a busy day or week, these meals are there for me. It takes the pressure and stress off of constantly having to plan a meal. If I need to deliver a meal, no problem, I just grab one out of my freezer.

I have been thrilled with the feedback from readers and customers of this book. This style of cooking has changed my life and enabled me to accomplish so much with the free time it saves me. I get countless emails from people telling me the same thing. I hope this book changes your life too!

grocery lists

Valencian Paella, Cumin-Cinnamon Beef Stew, Ginger-Cranberry Pork Roast

2 pounds boneless, skinless chicken breasts

2 pounds andouille sausage
 (or whatever kind of sausage you want)

4 pounds chuck roast
 or flank steak

2 pork roasts

2 cups frozen cooked shrimp

2 12-ounce packages fresh cranberries
 or 2 cans whole cranberries

8 cups red potatoes

6 cups baby carrots

2 cans (14.5 ounce each) diced tomatoes
 or 4 whole tomatoes

2 cups green beans or artichoke or peas

2 green bell peppers

1 fresh ginger root

salt

sweet paprika

saffron

chili powder

ground cumin

ground coriander

coarse salt

black pepper

ground cinnamon

cayenne pepper

Rapadura sugar

quick cooking tapioca
 or arrowroot flour

8 cups chicken broth

2 cups rice

Lamb & Lentil Stew, Opa's Empanadas, Summer Veggie Soup

8 lamb chops (about 4 pounds)

2 pounds ground beef

5 boiled eggs

pastry dough

2 large zucchinis

2 large yellow squash

4 cups corn kernels
 (cut from 4 ears fresh corn or frozen)

1 pound green beans

2 large red peppers

green olives

raisins

6 yellow onions

4 carrots

4 celery stalks

10 garlic cloves

2 cans (14 oz. each) diced tomatoes
 or 4 whole tomatoes

thyme

rosemary

salt

pepper

cumin

cayenne

bay leaves

2 15.5-ounce cans cannellini beans
 or about 3 cups dry

2 pounds lentils

12 cups chicken broth

parmesan cheese

4 pounds bone-in skinless chicken thighs
    (this is approximately 12 thighs)

7 medium onions

3 to 4 chopped jalapeno peppers

10 to 14 garlic cloves

2 red bell peppers

2 green bell peppers

1 large eggplant

4 medium sweet potatoes

1 lime

2 scallions

fresh ginger

cilantro

basil

4 bay leaves

cumin

curry powder

salt & pepper

5 pounds beef roast

4 packages whole Portobello mushrooms

4 cups beef broth

2 13.5-ounce cans coconut milk

brown sugar
    or Rapadura

soy sauce

2.5 cups dry black beans (about a pound)

Ginger-Cranberry Pork Roast

4 pounds flank steak

4 pounds chicken breasts or thighs

2 pounds carrots

2 shallots

green onions

3 medium apples

2 cans cranberry sauce

    or 2 bags cranberries

4 onions

2 lemons

2 cans diced tomatoes

    or 4 whole tomatoes

2 green peppers

2 red peppers

2 limes

6 cloves garlic

fresh ginger

salt

chili powder

cumin

coriander

olive oil or butter

quick cooking tapioca

    or arrowroot flour

raw, local honey

4 cups chicken broth

4 onions

3-4 pounds flank steak

4 pounds beef sirloin or rump roast

2 (2 ½ pound) whole/fryer chickens

12-14 garlic cloves

3 red bell peppers

cabbage

4 sweet potatoes

2 cans diced tomatoes

    or 4 whole tomatoes

2 bags frozen peas

6 carrots

4 celery stalks

1 big bunch kale

ginger

salt

pepper

basil

thyme

cayenne

A couple sprigs fresh parsley

4 bay leaves

Italian seasoning

    (homemade version: equal parts basil,

      marjoram, oregano, rosemary and thyme)

red pepper flakes

2 cups peanut butter

apple cider vinegar

chicken broth

beef broth

Moroccan Lamb Stew, Orange Beef, Chicken n' Cherries

4 pounds boneless lamb

3-4 pounds flank steak

4 to 5 pounds chicken breasts or strips
   or bone in thighs

3 onions

3 sweet potatoes

2 cans chopped tomatoes
or 4 whole tomatoes chopped

2 small bags baby carrots, about 2 cups

4 cans pitted cherries
   or 2 big bags fresh cherries

4 garlic cloves

8 green onions

cumin

red pepper flakes

bay leaves

thyme

coriander

cloves

raisins

orange juice

arrowroot flour
   or quick cooking tapioca

soy sauce

sugar

chili sauce

brown sugar

chicken broth

beef broth

Healthy Mama BBQ Chicken, Stephanie's Goulash, Chicken Curry

2-3 pounds beef stew meat

2-3 pounds chicken thighs or drumsticks

4 pounds chicken thighs or breasts

5 sweet potatoes

4 green bell peppers

1 red bell pepper

3 zucchinis

6 onions

12 cloves garlic

2 15-ounce cans tomato sauce
   or 4 whole tomatoes

4 beets

4 bags baby carrots

4 fresh mangos
   or 2 cans chopped mango

yellow mustard powder

salt

bay leaves

thyme

coriander

cloves

paprika

pepper

curry powder

cumin

4 6-ounce cans tomato paste

raisins

peanuts or cashews

1 cup chicken stock

quick cooking tapioca
   or arrowroot flour

brown sugar

egg noodles
   or squash spaghetti

worcestershire sauce

sour cream

Duck Stew, Pork and Butternut Squash, Sesame Honey Chicken

1 whole duck	2 cups honey
or 4 duck breasts	1 cup tamari sauce
2 pork roasts	4 teaspoons tapioca
(about 2 to 3 pounds each)	or arrowroot powder
6 pounds chicken breasts	1 to 2 tablespoons soaked and
or breast/thigh combo	dehydrated/roasted sesame seeds
3 cups filtered water	coconut oil
or duck/beef stock	bay leaves
5 carrots	sage
2 whole butternut squashes	thyme
3 celery sticks	Rapadura
1 onion	apple cider vinegar
2 shallots	salt
4 tablespoons garlic	pepper
10 oz tomato paste	red pepper flakes

Parmesan Chicken, Chicken Chili, Polynesian Chicken & Cilantro Lime Chicken

24 pounds chicken breasts

4 cups marinara sauce

2 cups fresh mozzarella

2 cups parmesan cheese

2 pastured eggs

2 pineapples

4 ears corn

4 whole tomatoes

    or 28 ounces canned diced tomatoes

3 red bell peppers

16 oz tomato paste

2 cups black beans

2 cups kidney beans

22 garlic cloves

4 tablespoons freshly grated ginger

2 cups fresh cilantro leaves

1 cup chicken broth

1 cup almond flour

4 tablespoons Bragg Liquid Aminos

4 tablespoons tapioca

    or arrowroot powder

1 cup honey

4 tablespoons lime juice

2 tablespoons shredded lime zest

salt

pepper

chili powder

garlic powder

onion powder

red pepper flakes

oregano

paprika

cumin

Beef Veggie Soup, Cajun Shrimp, Ginger Beef

9 pounds beef roast

4 pounds shrimp

8 tomatoes

12 carrots

4 sweet potatoes

4 medium onions

2 cups scallions

4 cups green bell pepper

2 cups red bell pepper

2 cups peas

2 cups sugar snap peas

14 garlic cloves

4 tablespoons grated fresh ginger

2 ½ cups filtered water

2 cups chicken broth

3 cups beef stock

    or filtered water

4 tablespoons tamari sauce

3 tablespoons tapioca

    or arrowroot powder

salt

pepper

thyme

parsley

bay leaves

onion powder

red pepper flakes

paprika

Hot-pepper sauce (optional)

4 pounds sausage

4 pounds flank steak

5 cups frozen shrimp

5 tablespoons butter

4 tomatoes

2 large onions

1 cup green onions

3 cups zucchini

2 cups diced green bell pepper

1 bag baby carrots

2 cups black beans

2 limes

2 cups cilantro

2 teaspoons fresh sage

12 cups kale leaves

2 cups lentils, preferably French green

16 tablespoons garlic

1 ½ cups red wine

red pepper flakes

salt

pepper

Argentine Beef Stew, Eggplant, Chickpea & Ground Beef Stir Fry

4 pounds beef stew
    or flank steak

2 pounds ground beef

2 teaspoons bacon grease

3 tablespoons butter

8 tomatoes

2 large eggplants
    (about 1 ½ pounds each)

2 pounds sweet potatoes

2 large onions

2 cups baby bella mushrooms

2 cups scallions

12 garlic cloves

4 tablespoons cilantro

½ cup fresh parsley

1 cup light beer

2 cups chickpeas

4 bay leaves

cumin

salt

pepper

oregano

cinnamon

Slow Cooker Recipes

True Valencian Paella is cooked with snails, chicken, and rabbit. Even though I lived in Valencia, Spain for a semester in college, I am not a fan of rabbit and snails. I mean, really, who is? If you are a fan of rabbits and snails, that's awesome, but it's not up my alley. So this is my lazy, snail-and-rabbit-free version. If you are a perfectionist about rice, you may want to cook it separately. I am never going for perfection, and cooking the rice in the slow cooker is just fine with me!

2 pounds boneless, skinless chicken breast
   halves, cut into 1 inch pieces

2 pounds andouille sausage
   (or whatever kind of sausage you want)
   cut into 1 inch pieces

2 14.5-ounce cans no salt added
   diced tomatoes or 4 whole tomatoes

2 cups green beans/artichoke/peas

2 green peppers, sliced big

3 teaspoons salt

3 teaspoons pepper

3 teaspoons sweet paprika

add day of cooking:

2 cups frozen cooked shrimp

A pinch of saffron

8 cups chicken broth

2 cups rice

Dump chicken breast and sausage into two separate gallon-sized freezer bags. Add tomatoes, green pepper, and your choice of beans, artichokes or peas. Then add salt, pepper and sweet paprika to your liking. Lay bag flat, label and place in your freezer.

The day of cooking, pull bag out of freezer and dump contents of bag into slow cooker. Add one cup of chicken broth.

Cook on low for 6 to 8 hours. After cooking for three hours, add in the rest of the chicken stock and the rice. Be sure to stir the rice in well, so it cooks evenly. Cook for another 3 hours, maybe more, maybe less, depending on your cooker.

Add in the shrimp and saffron the last thirty minutes of cooking.

Each bag makes about 6 to 8 servings. Calories, 419. Total fat, 12.5g. Protein, 25.3g. Fiber, 2.4g.

cumin-cinnamon beef stew

I love cumin and cinnamon together; it is one of my favorite combinations. I fell in love with cumin after taking an Ayurvedic cooking class before my daughter was born. When I make something with cinnamon, it brings such a warmth and happiness to the kitchen.

4 pounds chuck roast or flank steak

8 cups red potatoes, chopped

6 cups baby carrots

½ teaspoon chili powder

1 teaspoon ground cumin

½ teaspoon ground coriander

½ teaspoon coarse salt

½ teaspoon black pepper

1 teaspoon ground cinnamon

½ teaspoon cayenne pepper

A tiny pinch of sugar

add day of cooking:

1 cup filtered water

Mix spices together in one bowl and evenly distribute between two separate gallon-sized freezer bags. Then add veggies and meat. Mix up contents of bag a bit, lay flat, label and put in freezer.

Day of cooking, dump contents of bag into slow cooker, add the filtered water, and cook on low for 6 to 8 hours, or until fully cooked.

Each bag makes about 6 to 8 servings. Calories, 315. Total fat, 11g. Protein, 37.8g. Fiber, 1.8g.

ginger-cranberry pork roast

Tasted good - needed more sugar + less H2O

For the longest time, I couldn't cook to save my life. Instead, I stashed away recipes from books or magazines, copying them and jotting them down for the day when I had enough courage to try them. All those recipes patiently waited for me, until the day I felt like I was good enough to cook, when I was worthy to be in the kitchen and make good food for myself.

This is one of those recipes. Originally, this was a candied sauce to go with turkey but I modified it. Fresh ginger is so much healthier and tastier than candied ginger and it holds up well in a slow cooker. This is probably one of my favorite recipes. It makes a great leftover sandwich.

2 pork roasts

2 12-ounce packages fresh cranberries

    or 2 cans whole cranberries

1 cup peeled and grated fresh ginger

2 tablespoons Rapadura sugar

2 tablespoons quick cooking tapioca

    or arrowroot flour

add day of cooking:

1 cup filtered water

Combine all ingredients except water into two separate gallon-sized freezer bags. Lay flat, label and put in freezer.

Day of cooking dump contents of bag into slow cooker, add the water, and cook on low for 6 to 8 hours, or until fully cooked.

Serve with sautéed broccoli, cooked in lots of butter. I cook frozen broccoli this way, no need to thaw, just dump frozen broccoli into a hot pan with butter and it is delicious.

Each bag makes about 4 servings. Calories, 105. Total fat, 2.2g. Protein, 6.6g. Fiber, 1.8g.

lamb & lentil stew

I made this recipe for my first Easter with my husband. He is a church-goer-twice-a year kind of guy, so I try to make Easter and Christmas as special as possible in hopes that one day he will want to go to church with me more often! And of course I want to make a nice tradition for Penelope. I would love to overhear her one day telling a friend about this recipe and even better, having her make this one day for her family.

8 lamb chops, (about 4 pounds)

2 medium yellow onions, chopped

    (about two cups)

4 carrots, peeled and chopped

    (about 1 ½ cups)

4 celery stalks, chopped, (about 1 cup)

8 garlic cloves, peeled and chopped

2 cans (14 ounces) diced tomatoes

    or 2 fresh whole tomatoes, diced

2 pounds lentils (soaked overnight,

    1 pound per freezer bag)

4 cups chicken broth

4 teaspoons thyme

4 teaspoons rosemary

2 teaspoons salt

2 teaspoons pepper

add day of cooking:

parmesan cheese

Combine all ingredients into two separate gallon-sized freezer bags. Lay flat, label each bag, and place in your freezer.

Day of cooking, dump contents of bag into slow cooker and cook on high for 3 to 4 hours or low for 6 to 8. Sprinkle parmesan cheese to garnish when serving.

Each bag makes about 4 servings. Calories, 254. Total fat, 4.8g. Protein, 26.7g. Fiber, 12g.

opa's empanadas

My husband's parents are from Argentina, but they originally emigrated from Germany and Latvia. My mother-in-law's grandparents came to Argentina at the turn of the century from Germany (at the same time my great-grandparents were immigrating into Kansas from Germany) and my father-in-law's family came to Argentina in the late 40's. His family is Latvian and was escaping WWII. My husband's father, now called Opa (the German word for Grandpa) by my daughter, works on a ship over half the year. When he is home, he always makes a big batch of empanadas. These empanadas are amazing! They make such a great protein packed travel and snack food, I even like them cold.

2 pounds ground beef

2 large onions, chopped

2 large red peppers, chopped

5 boiled eggs, chopped

½ cup green olives

1 ½ cups raisins

pastry dough, cut in circles

1 ½ teaspoons cumin

1 teaspoon cayenne

1 teaspoon garlic

½ teaspoon salt

½ teaspoon pepper

Cook beef in slow cooker for 4 to 6 hours on high until cooked thoroughly. Then add the rest of the ingredients and cook for another 2 hours. Let cool.

Spoon mixture onto circle pastries and pinch them shut into the shape of half moons. If you don't have access to pre-made empanada pastry dough, the healthiest option is to make them from scratch so you can control the ingredients, or you can also use pre-made, packaged, frozen and thawed organic fillo/phyllo dough.

Freeze the empanadas on a cookie sheet for 1 hour (so they don't stick together), then put into gallon-sized freezer bags. Alternatively, you can simply freeze the beef mixture, and thaw it the day you make the empanadas.

Day of cooking, turn oven to 425 and cook for 35 minutes, until pastry is golden brown.

One serving is about 2 empanadas. Calories, 230. Total fat, 9.4g. Protein, 18.8g. Fiber, 1.3g.

summer veggie soup

Summer is when I stock up on locally farmed fruits and vegetables. I buy them in bulk at the peak of freshness and then I freeze them. They usually do not last me all year. Each year I buy more than the last and think surely I will make it this year, but it never happens! When you buy this way, you are supporting your local economy and saving money, because buying organic fruits and veggies in season is much, much cheaper (and they taste much better!).

If you wanted to add a protein to this soup, chicken or sausage would go great.

2 15.5-ounce cans cannellini beans
   or about 3 cups dry
   (be sure to soak overnight first)
2 large zucchinis
   cut into bite-sized pieces
2 large yellow squash
   cut into bite-sized pieces
1 pound green beans
   cut into bite-sized pieces

4 cups corn kernels
   (cut from 2 ears of corn or frozen)
2 medium onions, finely chopped
8 bay leaves
salt and pepper to taste

add day of cooking:

8 cups chicken stock

Combine all ingredients except stock into two separate gallon-sized freezer bags. Lay flat, label and place in freezer.

Day of cooking, dump contents of bag into slow cooker, add stock and cook on high for 2 to 3 hours or low for 5 to 6.

About 6 servings. Calories, 97. Total fat, 1.3g. Protein, 5.4g. Fiber, 3.7g.

Beans and rice are a great way to stretch your dollar. Good quality, organic beans and rice, usually bought in bulk, are affordable. This recipe is so tasty; I often make it alone, with no rice. I freeze the leftovers, in small, single-person portions. It makes a great, quick and nutritious lunch.

3 cups onions, chopped

3 to 4 jalapeno peppers, chopped

6 to 8 garlic cloves, chopped

4 bay leaves

1 tablespoon cumin

2 teaspoons salt

1 teaspoon pepper

add day of cooking:

2 ½ cups dry black beans

(about a pound)

enough filtered water to cover the

beans by two inches

Combine everything except beans in one gallon-sized freezer bag.

Day before cooking, soak beans overnight with lemon or whey.

Day of cooking, dump beans into slow cooker, add water and cover beans by two inches, then dump rest of ingredients into slow cooker. Cook on high 4 hours or on low 6 to 8.

Serve with rice or a salad. Add cilantro for garnish if you want.

Makes approximately 6 to 8 servings. Calories, 244. Total fat, 2g. Protein, 13g. Fiber, 14g.

thai chicken curry

I love all kinds of curry, and I love Thai food. This is a good combo of both! I can't wait 'til I can go to Thailand one day and taste real Thai food. Until then, this is a good fix!

4 pounds bone-in skinless chicken thighs
(about 12 thighs)

About 26 ounces coconut milk

2 tablespoons brown sugar

2 tablespoons soy sauce

2 medium onions, chopped

4 to 6 cloves garlic
finely chopped or grated

2-inch knob ginger
peeled and grated

2 red bell peppers
seeded and chopped

2 green bell peppers
seeded and chopped

1 large eggplant
peeled and cut into chunks

4 medium sweet potatoes

2 tablespoons curry powder

add day of cooking:

1 lime, cut into wedges (for garnish)

2 scallions, thinly sliced (for garnish)

½ cup chopped cilantro (for garnish)

½ cup chopped basil (for garnish)

Combine all ingredients, except garnish (lime, scallions, cilantro and basil), into two separate gallon-sized freezer bags. Label, lay flat and freeze.

Day of cooking, cook on high heat for about 4 hours on high or low for 6 to 8 hours or until the chicken is cooked through. Serve with rice.

Makes approximately 6 to 8 servings. Calories, 244. Total fat, 2g. Protein, 13g. Fiber, 14g.

penelope's carrot ginger soup

Penelope is a huge fan of soup. I am not sure why, since she is a pretty picky eater. But soup she digs. This, along with my Apple-Butternut Squash Soup is her favorite. This is not a slow cooker meal, but it freezes great. I usually portion 3 to 4 servings in a big a gallon freezer bag and several smaller 1 to 2 cup portions if I need something for myself for dinner when my husband is out of town.

2 pounds carrots peeled and chopped	1 teaspoon salt
4 tablespoons fresh ginger peeled and minced	½ teaspoon coriander
2 shallots, minced	1 tablespoon olive oil or 1 tablespoon butter
4 cups chicken broth	Thinly sliced green onions for topping

Heat the olive oil (or butter) over medium high heat. Add the minced shallot and sauté until tender, about five minutes. Add the ginger and sauté for another three-four minutes.

Add the chopped carrots, broth, coriander and salt and bring to a boil.

Reduce heat to simmer and cook for 10-15 minutes until carrots are tender. Carefully transfer to a blender and puree. Alternatively, if you have one of those fancy hand mixer thingies, that would work too!

Serve with thinly sliced green onions on top.

To freeze leftovers, ladle soup into freezer bags, a mix of portion sizes is a good idea, lay flat, label and place in freezer.

Makes approximately 6 to 8 servings. Calories, 220. Total fat, 7g. Protein, 9g. Fiber, 7g.

healing chicken soup

This is the perfect meal to bring to someone if they are in need of healing. Soup made with homemade broth is some of the most nutritious and nourishing food on the planet. And it is so easy to make! If you want to stretch your soup and make it a bit heartier, add about 2 cups of potatoes or pasta. But if you want this soup to be super duper healing, leave out the carbs.

2 onions, chopped

6 carrots, chopped
(about 2 cups)

4 celery stalks, chopped
(about 1½ cups)

2 cups kale, chopped

2 teaspoons salt

1 teaspoon pepper

1 teaspoon basil

1 teaspoon thyme

A couple sprigs fresh parsley

4 bay leaves

1 tablespoon apple cider vinegar

add day of cooking:

2 (2 ½ lb.) whole/fryer chickens

4 cups filtered water

Combine all ingredients, except water and chicken, into one gallon-sized freezer bag. Lay flat, label and place in freezer.

Day of cooking, dump into slow cooker. Add chicken (be sure to remove inards and giblets) and filtered water.

Cover and cook on low 8 to 10 hours (high 4 to 6 hours). One hour before serving, remove chicken and cool slightly. Remove meat from bones and return meat to crock pot. Serve with rice, noodles or a salad.

Makes approximately 6 to 8 servings. Calories, 343. Total fat, 21g. Protein, 31g. Fiber, 1g.

chicken n' cherries

4 to 5 pounds chicken breasts
or bone-in thighs

4 jars pitted cherries
or 2 bags fresh cherries
pitted, about 2 pounds

chili sauce

¼ cup brown sugar

2 tablespoons arrowroot flour

I used a couple tablespoons of chili sauce in each bag, because the sauce I buy is super spicy, add as much or as little as you want in accordance with your family's taste.

Assemble all ingredients into two separate gallon-sized freezer bags. Lay flat, label and place in freezer.

Day of cooking, dump contents of bag into slow cooker. Cook on low for 8 hours or on high for 4 hours. You can shred chicken if you want, or leave in chunks.

Serve with rice, cous-cous or salad. Makes great leftover sandwiches.

Approximately 8 servings. Calories, 364. Total fat, 4g. Protein, 65g. Fiber, 1g.

french dip beef stew

5 pounds beef roast

4 packages Portobello mushrooms

2 onions, chopped

add day of cooking:

4 cups beef broth

Combine all ingredients except broth into two separate one gallon-sized freezer bags. Lay flat, label and place in freezer.

Day of cooking, place contents of bag into slow cooker and add broth. Cook on low for 8 hours or on high for 4.

Serve with rice, cous-cous, a salad or make sandwiches.

This recipe makes extra liquid, for dipping if you make sandwiches.

Makes approximately 8. Calories, 351. Total fat, 12g. Protein, 54g. Fiber, 1g.

orange beef stew

3 to 4 pounds chuck roast

2 cups orange juice

2 tablespoons arrowroot flour

2 tablespoons soy sauce

1 tablespoon Rapadura sugar

4 tablespoons minced garlic

8 green onions, chopped

3 sweet potatoes, chopped

1 yellow onion, chopped

2 teaspoons thyme

2 teaspoons coriander

4 bay leaves

2 teaspoons cloves

2 tablespoons quick-cooking tapioca
or arrowroot flour

add day of cooking:

2 cups beef broth

Combine all ingredients except beef broth into two separate gallon-sized freezer bags.
Lay flat, label and place in your freezer.

Day of cooking, place contents of bag into your slow cooker and add beef broth. Cook on low for 8 hours or on high for 4.

Serve with rice, cous-cous, a salad or make sandwiches.

Makes approximately 10 servings. Calories, 461. Total fat, 17g. Protein, 52g. Fiber, 2g.

cranberry chicken

4 pounds chicken breasts or thighs

3 medium apples, cut into wedges

2 medium onions, chopped

The juice of two lemons

2 tablespoons quick cooking tapioca

    or arrowroot flour

2 tablespoons honey

2 cans cranberry sauce

    or 2 bags fresh cranberries

Combine all ingredients into two separate gallon-sized freezer bags. Lay flat, label and place in freezer.

Day of cooking, dump contents of bag into slow cooker and cook on high for 3 hours or low for 6.

Serve with rice, couscous or a salad.

Makes approximately 8 servings. Calories, 226. Total fat, 2g. Protein, 26g. Fiber, 2g.

moroccan lamb stew

4 pounds boneless lamb

2 large onions, chopped

2 cans chopped tomatoes

    or 4 whole tomatoes, chopped

2 cups carrots, chopped

    or 2 bags baby carrots

2 teaspoons ground cumin

2 teaspoons red pepper flakes

1 cup raisins

add day of cooking:

2 cups chicken broth

Assemble all ingredients except broth into two separate gallon-sized freezer bags. Lay flat, label and place in freezer.

Day of cooking, dump contents of bag into slow cooker and cook on high for 4 hours or low for 8 hours.

Serve with rice, couscous or salad.

Makes approximately 8 servings. Calories, 405. Total fat, 27g. Protein, 21g. Fiber, 2g.

italian beef

4 pounds beef sirloin or rump roast, cubed

2 tablespoons Italian seasoning

    (homemade version: equal parts basil,

    marjoram, oregano, rosemary and thyme)

2 teaspoons red pepper flakes

6 to 8 garlic cloves, minced

3 red peppers, thinly sliced

add day of cooking:

2 cups beef broth

Combine all ingredients except stock into two separate gallon-sized freezer bags. Lay flat, label and place in freezer.

Day of cooking, dump contents of bag into slow cooker and cook on high for 4 hours or on low for 8 hours.

Serve with rice, couscous, or a salad. You could even use this as a pizza topping (add cheese of course). Leftovers make great sandwiches.

Makes approximately 8 servings. Calories, 397. Total fat, 19g. Protein, 48g. Fiber, 1g.

peanut stew

3 to 4 pounds flank steak

2 large onions, chopped

6 cloves garlic, chopped

3 tablespoons fresh ginger, minced

½ head cabbage, chopped

4 sweet potatoes, chopped

2 cans diced tomatoes with liquid,
    or 4 whole tomatoes, chopped

2 cups chicken broth

2 teaspoons salt

2 teaspoons cayenne pepper

add day of cooking:

2 bags frozen peas

2 cups peanut butter

Combine ingredients except peas and peanut butter into two separate gallon-sized freezer bags. Lay flat, label and place in freezer.

Day of cooking, dump contents of bag into slow cooker and cook on high for 4 hours or on low for 8 hours. Add the bag of frozen peas and peanut butter the last thirty minutes of cooking.

Makes approximately 8 to 10 servings. Calories, 391. Total fat, 20g. Protein, 29g. Fiber, 6g.

flank steak fajitas

4 pounds flank steak

2 large onions, chopped

2 green bell peppers, chopped

2 red bell peppers, chopped

6 cloves garlic, minced

2 cans diced tomatoes

    or 4 whole tomatoes, chopped

2 teaspoons chili powder

2 teaspoons cumin

2 teaspoons coriander

1 teaspoon salt

add day of cooking:

lime juice (for garnish)

Combine all ingredients into two separate gallon-sized freezer bags. Lay flat, label and place in freezer.

Day of cooking, dump contents of bag into slow cooker and cook on high for 4 hours or on low for 8 hours.

Serve with tortillas, shredded cheese, guacamole, sour cream and salsa.

Makes approximately 6 to 8 servings. Calories, 200. Total fat, 8g. Protein, 25g. Fiber, 2g.

healthy mama bbq chicken

2 to 3 pounds chicken thighs or drumsticks

3 medium sweet potatoes
  (peeled or unpeeled), cut into
  ½ inch pieces (about 2 cups)

2 large green peppers
  cut into strips or cubes (about 2 cups)

1 large red pepper
  cut into strips or cubes (about 1 cup)

2 zucchinis, chopped (about 2 cups)

2 cups chopped onion

2 tablespoons quick-cooking tapioca
  or arrowroot flour

2 15-ounce jars tomato sauce

4 tablespoons brown sugar

2 tablespoons Worcestershire sauce

2 tablespoons ground yellow mustard

6 cloves garlic finely minced

1 teaspoon salt

Combine all ingredients into two separate one gallon-sized freezer bags. Lay flat, label and place in freezer.

Day of cooking, dump contents of bag into slow cooker and cook on high for 4 hours or on low for 8 hours.

Makes approximately 8 to 10 servings. Calories, 279. Total fat, 9g. Protein, 21g. Fiber, 5g.

stephanie's goulash

2 to 3 pounds beef stew meat

3 cups onions, chopped

2 ½ cups green bell peppers, chopped

4 large beets, peeled and chopped
   (about 2 cups)

2 cups baby carrots
   or chopped carrots

4 cloves garlic, minced

4 6-ounce cans tomato paste

2 tablespoons paprika

1 teaspoon ground black pepper

add day of cooking:

4 cups hot cooked egg noodles
   (or squash spaghetti for a
   gluten-free version)

½ cup dairy sour cream (for garnish)

Combine all ingredients except noodles and sour cream into two separate one gallon-sized freezer bags. Lay flat, label and place in freezer.

Day of cooking, dump contents of bag into slow cooker and cook on high for 4 hours or on low for 8 hours. Cook noodles separately, use sour cream as garnish.

Makes approximately 8 to 10 servings. Calories, 418. Total fat, 21g. Protein, 28g. Fiber, 7g.

chicken curry

4 pounds chicken thighs or breasts
cut into 1 inch pieces

3 tablespoons arrowroot flour

4 tablespoons curry powder

2 teaspoons ground cumin

2 cups sweet potatoes, chopped

2 cups baby carrots

4 cups coarsely chopped mango
or 2 cans chopped mango

1 cup chopped onion

1 zucchini chopped (about 1 cup)

2 cloves garlic, minced

2 bay leaves

1 teaspoon thyme

1 teaspoon coriander

1 teaspoon cloves

add day of cooking:

1 cup chicken stock

½ cup raisins (for garnish)

½ cup peanuts or cashews (for garnish)

Combine all ingredients except raisins and peanuts into two separate gallon-sized freezer bags. Lay flat, label and place in freezer.

Day of cooking, dump contents of bag into slow cooker, add chicken stock and cook on high for 4 hours or on low for 8 hours. Use raisins and peanuts as garnish.

Makes approximately 6 to 8 servings. Calories, 310. Total fat, 6g. Protein, 30g. Fiber, 4g.

duck stew

1 whole duck
   or 4 duck breasts, cubed
3 cups filtered water
   or duck/beef stock
1 tablespoon Rapadura (optional)
2 teaspoons apple cider vinegar

5 carrots, chopped
3 celery sticks, chopped
2 whole shallots, chopped
2 bay leaves
1 tablespoon sage
1 teaspoon salt and pepper, or to taste

If using duck breasts, cube and place into freezer bag. If using a whole duck, freeze whole and add to the slow cooker the day of cooking. Chop veggies and assemble into one freezer bag. Lay flat, label and place in freezer.

Day of cooking, place ingredients in your slow cooker and cook on low for 8 hours.

Once the whole duck is cooked, remove from slow cooker and take meat off the bone. This meal can be eaten in several ways: return the meat to the slow cooker to eat as a stew/soup, or serve the duck with a side of veggies (save the stock for cooking with later!) and rice or fresh salad.

Each bag makes about 8-10 servings. Calories, 539. Total fat, 50g. Protein, 16g. Fiber, 1g.

pork and butternut squash

2 pork roasts
(about 2 to 3 pounds each)
2 whole butternut squashes
cut into one inch cubes

2 tablespoons dried thyme
4 tablespoons garlic, minced
1 teaspoon salt and pepper, or to taste

Leaving the skin on, chop butternut squash into one inch cubes. Divide squash and spices into two separate gallon-sized freezer bags, along with one pork roast in each. Lay flat, label and place in your freezer.

Day of cooking, place contents of bag into slow cooker and cook on high for 3 hours or on low for 6 hours. Serve with white rice or a fresh green salad.

Each bag makes about 4-6 servings. Calories, 307. Total fat, 17g. Protein, 27g. Fiber, 2g.

sesame honey chicken

6 pounds chicken breasts
   or breast/thigh combo

1 onion, chopped (about one cup)

10 ounces tomato paste

2 cups honey

1 cup tamari sauce

1 to 2 tablespoons sesame seeds
   soaked and dehydrated/roasted

2 tablespoons coconut oil

1 teaspoon red pepper flakes

4 teaspoons tapioca
   or arrowroot powder

2 teaspoons salt and pepper, or to taste

Chop chicken into one inch cubes. Divide into two separate gallon-sized freezer bags, along with the rest of ingredients except sesame seeds. Lay flat, label and place in freezer.

Day of cooking, place contents of bag into slow cooker and cook on low for 6 to 8 hours or on high for 3 to 4 hours. Sprinkle with sesame seeds and serve with white rice.

Each bag makes about 6-8 servings. Calories, 625. Total fat, 29g. Protein, 27g. Fiber, 3g.

parmesan chicken

6 pounds chicken breasts

2 cups sliced fresh mozzarella

   (or shredded if you don't have fresh)

1 cup parmesan cheese

2 eggs

2 jars marinara sauce (about 4 cups)

1 cup almond flour

1 teaspoon salt and pepper, or to taste

Beat eggs in a bowl. Dip chicken into the egg mixture and put chicken into two separate gallon-sized freezer bags, splitting the chicken evenly between the two bags. In another bowl, mix flour, parmesan cheese, salt, and pepper. Add half of the flour mixture to each bag and close up the bag. Shake the bag to coat the chicken evenly.

Day of cooking, add some marinara sauce to the bottom of the slow cooker, then add the chicken breasts. Then add mozzarella and then more marinara sauce. Repeat this process until all of chicken, cheese and marinara sauce is in the slow cooker.

Cook on low for 6 to 8 hours, or on high for 3 hours. Serve with a fresh green salad or sauteed veggies.

Each bag makes about 6-8 servings. Calories, 659. Total fat, 40g. Protein, 37g. Fiber, 4g.

chicken chili

6 pounds chicken breasts	1 teaspoon garlic powder
2 cups black beans	1 teaspoon onion powder
2 cups kidney beans	1 teaspoon red pepper
4 ears corn	1 teaspoon oregano
16 ounces tomato paste	1 teaspoon paprika
28 ounces diced tomatoes	2 teaspoons cumin
(or 4 whole tomatoes, diced)	1 teaspoon salt and pepper, or to taste
2 tablespoons chili powder	

Split all ingredients except beans into two separate gallon-sized freezer bags. Lay flat, label and place in freezer.

Night before cooking, soak beans overnight.

Day of cooking, place soaked beans and contents of bag into slow cooker and cook on low for 6 to 8 hours or on high for 3 to 4 hours. Serve with white rice or a fresh green salad.

Each bag makes about 6-8 servings. Calories, 649. Total fat, 27g. Protein, 38g. Fiber, 13g.

polynesian chicken

6 pounds chicken breasts

3 red bell peppers, cored, seeded
and sliced into one inch strips

2 whole pineapples, cut into chunks

6 cloves garlic, minced

4 tablespoons freshly grated ginger

1 cup honey

4 tablespoons Bragg Liquid Aminos

4 tablespoons tapioca
or arrowroot powder

1 teaspoon salt and pepper, or to taste

Split ingredients into two separate gallon-sized freezer bags. Lay flat, label and place in freezer.

Day of cooking, place contents of bag into slow cooker and cook on low for 6 to 8 hours or on high for 3 to 4 hours.

Serve with white rice, green salad or sauteed veggies.

Each bag makes about 6-8 servings. Calories, 583. Total fat, 27g. Protein, 26g. Fiber, 4g.

beef veggie soup

5 pounds beef roast

6 medium carrots

    cut into 1-inch-thick slices

4 sweet potatoes

    cut into 1-inch cubes

2 medium onions, chopped

2 cups peas

1 teaspoon salt and pepper, or to taste

2 teaspoons dried thyme

2 tablespoons garlic, minced

4 bay leaves

4 whole tomatoes, chopped

2 teaspoons dried parsley

2 cups filtered water

Split all ingredients except peas into two separate gallon-sized freezer bags. If peas are already frozen, just leave them in the original bag and add the day of cooking. If they are fresh, place them in a separate small freezer bag and place inside larger bag. Lay flat, label and place in freezer. You can dump them in with everything if you want, they will just be a bit less mushy if you add the peas separately the last thirty minutes of cooking.

Day of cooking, place contents of bags into slow cooker, except peas, and cook on low for 6 to 8 hours or on high for 3 to 4 hours, add peas the last thirty minutes of cooking. Serve with white rice or a fresh green salad.

Each bag makes about 6-8 servings. Calories, 414. Total fat, 27g. Protein, 29g. Fiber, 3g.

4 pounds shrimp

    shelled and deveined

4 whole tomatoes, chopped

4 cups onions, chopped

4 cups green bell pepper, chopped

6 garlic cloves, minced

½ cup filtered water

2 cups chicken broth

Hot-pepper sauce (optional)

1 teaspoon onion powder

1 teaspoon red pepper flakes

1 teaspoon paprika

1 teaspoon salt and black pepper

Split ingredients into two separate gallon-sized freezer bags. Lay flat, label and place in freezer.

Day of cooking, place contents of bag into slow cooker and cook on low for 6 to 8 hours or on high for 3 to 4 hours.

Serve with white rice or a fresh green salad.

Each bag makes about 3-4 servings. Calories, 331. Total fat, 5g. Protein, 50g. Fiber, 3g.

ginger beef

4 pounds beef roast

    (either leave bone-in or cut

    into 1-inch cubes)

6 carrots

    cut into 1-inch-thick slices

2 cups scallions, sliced

2 cups chopped red bell pepper

2 cups sugar snap peas

6 garlic cloves, minced

4 tablespoons grated fresh ginger

3 cups beef stock

    (or if using bone-in roast,

    use 3 cups filtered water)

4 tablespoons tamari sauce

2 teaspoons red pepper flakes

3 tablespoons tapioca

    or arrowroot powder

1 teaspoon salt and pepper, or to taste

Split all ingredients except sugar snap peas into two separate gallon-sized freezer bags. If sugar snap peas are already frozen leave them in original bag and add them the day of cooking. If they are fresh, place them in a separate small freezer bag and place inside larger bag. Lay flat, label and place in freezer.

Day of cooking, place contents of the larger freezer bag (all ingredients except sugar snap peas) into slow cooker and cook on low for 6 to 8 hours or on high for 3 to 4 hours. Add sugar snap peas for the last thirty minutes of cooking. Serve with white rice or a fresh green salad.

Each bag makes about 4-6 servings. Calories, 433. Total fat, 28g. Protein, 32g. Fiber, 2g.

cilantro lime chicken

6 pounds large chicken breasts

1 cup shredded parmesan cheese

8 tablespoons garlic, chopped

4 tablespoons lime juice

2 tablespoons shredded lime zest

1 cup chicken broth

1 teaspoon salt and pepper, or to taste

2 teaspoons garlic powder

2 cups fresh cilantro leaves

(do not include stems)

Split all ingredients except cilantro into two separate gallon-sized freezer bags. Place cilantro into smaller freezer bag and place inside larger bag. Lay flat, label and place in freezer.

Day of cooking, place contents of larger freezer bag (all ingredients except cilantro) into slow cooker and cook on low for 6 to 8 hours or on high for 3 to 4 hours. Add cilantro for the last thirty minutes of cooking. Serve with white rice, green salad or sauteed veggies, or put into taco shells or sprouted tortillas and serve with taco garnishes (salsa, sour cream, shredded cheese, avocado, etc).

Each bag makes about 6-8 servings. Calories, 505. Total fat, 30g. Protein, 30g. Fiber, 2g.

One Dish Recipes

kale, sausage & lentil skillet dinner

4 pounds sausage

3 teaspoons butter

2 large onions, thinly sliced

12 cups kale leaves, chopped
  (with tough stems removed)

6 tablespoons garlic, chopped

2 tablespoons red pepper flakes

2 cups lentils
  (preferably French green)

2 ½ cups water

1 ½ cups red wine

2 teaspoons fresh sage, chopped

2 teaspoons salt

Freshly ground pepper, to taste

To assemble, split all ingredients except kale, water, wine, and lentils into two separate gallon-sized freezer bags. Place kale into smaller freezer bag and place inside larger bag. Lay flat, label and place in freezer.

Day of cooking, heat one teaspoon of butter in a large cast iron skillet over medium heat. Add sausages and cook until browned on all sides, 4 to 5 minutes total. Transfer to a clean cutting board.

Add the remaining butter and the rest of the vegetables and spices. Add water and wine, ncrease heat to high and bring to a boil, scraping up any browned bits. Add lentils, reduce heat to maintain a simmer, and cook partially covered for 40 minutes. Slice the sausage and stir into the pan. Cover and cook until heated through, about 2 minutes.

Each bag makes about 6-8 servings. Calories, 521. Total fat, 33g. Protein, 29g. Fiber, 9g.

cilantro lime shrimp skillet dinner

5 cups frozen shrimp
(shelled and deveined)

1 bag baby carrots

2 cups cilantro

6 tablespoons garlic, minced

add day of cooking:

juice of 2 limes

1 to 2 tablespoons butter

To assemble the meals for freezing, dump shrimp, cilantro and garlic into two separate gallon-sized freezer bags. Divide bag of carrots into two smaller bags and place one inside each of the larger bags. Lay flat, label and place in freezer.

Day of cooking, cook carrots first, placing in cast iron skillet with enough water to just barely cover the carrots. Boil and add butter as the water evaporates completely and the carrots are soft. Once carrots are cooked, transfer to a plate and set aside.

Put a dollop of butter in skillet and add garlic, shrimp and cilantro. Cook for about 4 minutes until shrimp is cooked thoroughly. Add the juice of one lime and mix together.

Serve immediately with side of carrots.

Each bag makes about 3-4 servings. Calories, 206. Total fat, 8g. Protein, 29g. Fiber, 1g.

zucchini, black bean & steak fajitas

4 pounds flank steak

2 tablespoons butter

3 cups zucchini
   (quartered lengthwise, and sliced)

2 cups diced green bell pepper

4 tomatoes, diced

4 tablespoons garlic

1 cup green onions

2 cups black beans

Split all ingredients except beans into two separate gallon-sized freezer bags. Lay flat, label and place in freezer.

Night before cooking, soak beans overnight.

Day of cooking, heat a cast iron skillet and add butter. Put in garlic, green onions, soaked beans, zucchini, bell peppers, and tomatoes, saute for about 8 minutes, and set aside. Add a little bit more butter and saute the flank steak until cooked to your liking.

Serve with fajitas garnishes (salsa, sour cream, shredded cheese, avocado, etc).

Each bag makes about 4-6 servings. Calories, 385. Total fat, 13g. Protein, 40g. Fiber, 7g.

argentine beef stew

4 pounds beef stew or flank steak

2 cups scallions, chopped

2 pounds sweet potatoes
  (cut into one inch cubes)

6 cloves garlic, minced

4 tomatoes, chopped

2 teaspoons bacon grease

1 cup light beer

1 cup water

4 tablespoons cilantro, minced

2 teaspoons cumin

2 teaspoons salt

2 bay leaves

1 teaspoon pepper

To assemble, divide all ingredients except bacon grease into two separate gallon-sized bags. Lay flat, label and place in freezer.

Day of cooking, use a large cast iron skillet to heat bacon grease over medium heat. Add scallions, garlic, tomatoes, cilantro, and a pinch of salt and cook about 4 to 5 minutes, constantly stirring.

Add beef to the pot along with beer, water, cumin, bay leaves, and salt, if needed. Cover and simmer on low heat for 1 ½ hours. Add potatoes and cook until soft, about 20 more minutes.

Each bag makes about 3-4 servings. Calories, 484. Total fat, 17g. Protein, 50g. Fiber, 5g.

eggplant, chickpea & ground beef stirfry

2 pounds ground beef

3 tablespoons butter

2 cups baby bella mushrooms

2 large eggplants

   (about 1 ½ pounds each)

2 large onions, thinly sliced

4 tomatoes chopped

½ cup finely chopped fresh parsley

6 tablespoons garlic, minced

2 cups chickpeas, rinsed,

   (soaked overnight and drained)

2 teaspoons dried oregano, crumbled

2 teaspoons cinnamon

2 teaspoons salt

2 teaspoons pepper

2 bay leaves

To assemble, put all ingredients except butter into two separate gallon-sized freezer bags. Lay flat, label and place in freezer.

Night before cooking, rinse and soak chickpeas overnight and drain.

Day of cooking, using a large cast iron skillet, heat butter over medium heat. Add ground beef, cook through and set aside, leaving the fat in the skillet. In same cast iron skillet, saute mushrooms, onions, eggplants, chickpea, and spices until soft. Add beef back in and mix together. Serve with white rice or a fresh green salad.

Each bag makes about 4-6 servings. Calories, 342. Total fat, 15g. Protein, 24g. Fiber, 10g.

Notes

notes

notes

notes

notes

notes

acknowledgements

This book would not be possible without several people. Big thanks to Lindsey Morrow from Mother Rising blog (MotherRisingBirth.com) for introducing me to the blog, Once A Month Mom and the idea freezer cooking in the first place. Tricia, Once a Month Mom herself (OnceAMonthMom.com), is now a good friend of mine and I would like to thank her for giving me the inspiration to come up with my slow cooker freezer recipes. If I hadn't started doing once a month cooking, I would have never of had my Big Idea. And for her helping me taking the leap into writing an cookbook. She has been so helpful in pointing me in the right direction for resources and information.

Huge thanks to Kim Williams of the The Polka Dot Press (ThePolkaDotPress.com) for designing the super cute recipe labels.

Big thanks to Renee Whiting of Nana's Empty Nest (ReneeWhiting.com) for taking some of the pictures featured in this book. My food photography skills are lacking and she saved the day!

I would like to thank Cassandra Roy for being my right hand gal. Her attention to detail and hard work has helped this cookbook come to fruition. Also, Jessica of The Pixelista (ThePixelista.com). She is the technical wizard behind my blog. She patiently answers five million emails from me and makes this all possible. Without Jessica this book would not look as amazing as it does. And Leslee Boldman, my editor extraordinaire. She is my sounding board and her ability to concentrate on details for long periods of time astounds me.

To my husband Peter, who has supported my blog and now this cookbook. At first he thought blogging was a joke, but now he has my back.

And of course, to my sweet Penelope, the love of my life and my inspiration and motivation for everything I do.

Made in the USA
Charleston, SC
30 December 2012